Marriage Go Round

Basic Workbook

**Nine Steps to Improving Your Relationship
and Rekindling Love in Your Life**

F. Russell Crites, Jr.

© 2015 Floyd Russell Crites, Jr.

Published by CPC Publications

Cover Design by Tigerlilly

First Printing, November 2015

Printed in the United States of America

Some of the worksheets that are in this workbook have been a result of information that has been collected over the years. As a result, there is no way in which I can give credit where credit is due. However, I do want to give a general thank you to all my professors, mentors and fellow therapists and clients who have given me the input necessary to put this material together.

Crites, Floyd Russell, Jr.

Marriage Go Round Workbook

1. Marriage Therapy, 2. Couple Therapy 3. Man-woman relationships, 4. Communication in Marriage

A Special Thank You

Over the years I have had the privilege of being asked to present a number of programs regarding marriage or relationships. At many of these programs I have asked therapists and couples to write down exercises, strategies, etc. that have helped them address any issue of importance in the past in some way. As a result, I have received hundreds of suggestions over the years. In addition to the many researched based methods, I have included some of those exercises I have received over the years. I have no way of acknowledging who gave these to me. However, I am deeply thankful for the creativity and I wish I could give credit where credit is due. Since I can't, I just want to say 'Thank you' for all of the creative, wonderful techniques that were shared. I hope that you find these as useful as I have over the years.

The strategies, techniques and information in this workbook are meant to be used by a licensed mental health professional who has been trained in marriage therapy. They are not intended as a substitute for counseling with a mental health provider. In addition, this is being sold with the understanding that neither the author nor the publisher is engaged in rendering psychological advice or diagnosis which should only be done in a therapeutic environment. Neither the author, nor the publisher shall be liable for any loss, injury, or damage allegedly arising from any information or suggestions in this workbook.

Marriage Go Round
Introduction

This workbook seeks to present a system of conceptualization regarding the life-cycle of a love relationship and how therapeutic intervention can take place. The assumption is made that change is the normal state of any relationship. Some changes are negative in nature and destructive of the relationship. Other changes are positive and contribute to the relationship in which they take place. It is the energy of this change which has the potential of creating a synergistic environment in which the potential for successful happy living of the couple together exceeds the potential of each individual.

The Relationship Cycle that is found within will help you gauge where you are in your relationship. Having used the model as a diagnostic tool, it is then possible to use it as a road map for planning how you can improve or rekindle your love relationship. It is very useful in setting the goals for a therapy contract, tracing progress, and knowing when to terminate counseling.

There is a limitation to this work. The Relationship Process and the forms that support it are tools for counseling. It deals with education, expectations and perceptions. It also assumes that you 'want' to change to improve your relationship. In other words, it deals with first order changes that happen in the conscious mind. If one or both of you are dealing with a psychodynamic disorder that could limit your ability to deal rationally with the issues, a more in-depth approach is needed to achieve a second order change. This would require a deeper, more therapeutic level of 'therapy' and should be accomplished before attempting to utilize first order change as outlined in the therapists manual and this workbook.

As defined in this workbook, counseling seeks to teach you better ways to perceive the inevitable changes that come into your relationship. It will also help you learn new coping mechanisms, and how to practice principles for a healthy relationship.

However, in many cases strategies and techniques such as those found in this workbook are not adequate by themselves and additional material may be offered in order to meet your specific needs. If you are working with a therapist who recommended this workbook (s)he will have access to a multitude of individual and couple worksheets, handouts, strategies, etc. Having access to these resources will help address your specific issues in a more thorough way.

I wish you a wonderful journey as you seek to improve and rekindle love in your life.

F. Russell Crites, M.S., LPC, LMFT, LSSP, NBCCH, CPC

TABLE OF CONTENTS

Therapy Contract

You have chosen to come to a professional to seek help concerning your relationship. This shows that you are concerned and desire positive change. However, making such changes is often very difficult even when the changes are positive in nature. Ridding yourself of negative behaviors is even more difficult, and as a result painful. Often when change begins in relationships things get worse before they get better. This is because you are opening old wounds in order for them to heal properly. Don't worry, when things seem the worse that means that we are ready to take positive strides forward.

To make therapy work you must be willing to change your behavior so that it will promote wellness in your relationship. You must believe that your therapist will guide you in a direction that will promote positive growth. This will be accomplished by helping you understand self and partner, setting goals, and enacting the behaviors that are necessary for you to attain that which you desire. For therapy to be effective you must commit to the following:

- Attend and participate in at least twelve sessions with your partner

- Do all assigned homework between sessions

- Make no decision to negatively alter the situation or relationship unless you are in a therapy situation

At the end of twelve sessions both you and your therapist will evaluate your situation to determine what else needs to be done to accomplish what you want in therapy. It may be that you have resolved the problems, or that you still have some changing to do before you will be happy. You may have come to a realization that you will have to either accept the situation as it is, or change it. Whatever the case you should know for sure what would be best in the situation at the end of twelve sessions. It is at this point that you and your therapist will determine whether or not you need to continue in therapy.

If you are willing to commit to the conditions as outlined above for therapy then please sign your name below.

Name:_____ Date:_____

My Concerns

Worksheet

What I Can Do to Improve Self and Our Relationship	
To Remove or Reduce for Self	**To Increase or Begin for Self**
To Remove or Reduce for my Relationship	**To Increase or Begin for my Relationship**

What My Partner Can Do to Improve Self and Our Relationship	
To Remove or Reduce for Self	**To Increase or Begin for Self**
To Remove or Reduce for the Relationship	**To Increase or Begin for the Relationship**

Name:_____ **Date:**_____

Instructions: Look at each of the potential issues listed below and rate whether or not each one is an issue in any way for you or your partner in your relationship. You are not rating your partner. You are rating if any of these areas are causing a problem for either of you in the relationship. There are empty spots at the end. If you have concerns that are not listed you may add them to this list.

1 = No problem   2 = Mild Problem   3 = Moderate Problem   4 = Significant Problem

	Relationship Concerns	Area Defined	Rating
1	Change, a willingness to change self	There must be a willingness to change as life occurs in a relationship, This is not changing your personality. It is looking within, or by listening to others, so that you can identify ways that you can become a better person, how you can become a better partner.	1 2 3 4
2	Anger, Past Hurts and Irritants	Anger can cause significant difficulties in a relationship, as can past hurts and everyday irritants. It is essential that each person learn how to address these issues in his/her life and learn to be supportive of his/her partner as these issues are addressed.	1 2 3 4
3	Conflict Resolution or Management	Problems and problem solving are just a normal part of life. We come to a resolution or compromise with our disagreements.	1 2 3 4
4	Forgiveness and Reconciliation	Forgiving others is important if you are to heal or at least improve a relationship. It is also important that you learn how to get forgiveness when you have offended someone. Learning to make recompense for reconciliation is important.	1 2 3 4
5	Emotional Connection	Being emotionally connected calls for each person to identify what triggers positive emotional feelings in his/her partner and then do all you can to make sure those things happen often. Any positive emotional experience will cause you to feel closer to your partner.	1 2 3 4
6	Commitment to Partner	Each person in the relationship has resolved to make the relationship work and is willing to make some sacrifices and take the steps needed to keep their relationship moving forward even when times are rough.	1 2 3 4
7	Priorities, Partner	If you are to have a healthy relationship you must put your partner before children, personal time, work, friends, etc. Some people acknowledge that the only thing that should be above their partner is GOD.	1 2 3 4
8	Service Love	Serving your partner is really about developing an awareness of your partner's needs (how they are being overwhelmed at that given moment), and making a decision without being asked to simply help out. The underlying purpose of serving your partner is to show your love by making his/her life easier at that specific moment in time.	1 2 3 4

9	Admiration	You show admiration to someone who has positive characteristics worthy of adoration, love or respect. Admiration is a great motivator. When it is expressed it often is seen as a reward for well-doing or well-being.	1 2 3 4
10	Affection, Non-Sexual	Touching, hugs, holding hands, stroking hair, etc. are expressions of affection. Any non-sexual bonding experience that both enjoy, or that you can do to make your spouse feel loved and special.	1 2 3 4
11	Appreciation	You can show appreciation for your partner as you see them use their abilities for good or when they have done something for you or others. This can be done by patting them on the back, a gentle touch, a verbal thank you (be specific what it's for).	1 2 3 4
12	Attractive Partner	Most people like to spend time with people who are attractive and who do their best to look good. Looks aren't everything, but they are important for many people. How you look is often a reflection of your self-image. Men, being more visual, often need to have partners who take good care of themselves.	1 2 3 4
13	Commitment to Family	Both partners want the other to be a good mother, father and spouse. Putting the family first is often hard but essential if a family is to be healthy.	1 2 3 4
14	Communication, Verbal	As human beings we all need communication. In most cases women need conversation in a relationship more than men do. It is very important that you take time to talk to each other on a daily basis.	1 2 3 4
15	Domestic Support	Either one or both people in a relationship may have a need to be helped regarding routine household duties. It should be an equal sharing of duties outside and inside when both work.	1 2 3 4
16	Emotional Security	Knowing that your spouse will protect you from emotional harm. This also means that your partner will seek not to emotionally abuse you but rather lift you up as an important person in his/her life.	1 2 3 4
17	Finances	You have an agreement about how to spend money, how to pay the bills, how to save and how much each of you have for personal spending.	1 2 3 4
18	Focused Attention	Focused attention simply means that when you are with your partner you focus on him/her. You listen, laugh, empathize, and generally make sure that (s)he knows that at that moment in time (s)he is the most important thing in the world to you	1 2 3 4
19	Fun and Common Interests (having a recreational partner and friendships for socialization)	Having fun with someone you like being with is very bonding emotionally. It's important that you spend time having fun together. When you share common interests that both of you love doing it becomes even more positive and bonding for you in your relationship. This also includes the need for friendships to stimulate the relationship.	1 2 3 4
20	Goals, Marital	Together you have set goals for your marriage and you have worked toward those goals as a team.	1 2 3 4
21	Honesty	Honesty is the act of saying the truth whenever you are asked for it. Honesty never hides, it is an open book. However, honesty should also be gentle and kind.	1 2 3 4

22	Listening	Listening occurs when you, 1) listen for meaning or what your partner is trying to communicate, and 2) when you try to understand and see where your spouse is coming from, what they are thinking, and why they feel the way they do.	1 2 3 4
23	Openness	Openness occurs as you share what is going on inside of you as well as what has happened to you or around you on a day-by-day basis. Nothing should be hidden or kept from your partner. However, just as with honesty it should be shared in a gentle and kind way.	1 2 3 4
24	Personal Space	Everyone needs time alone! Time for relaxation, reading or simply enjoying a bath are essential if a person is going to feel good about self and have healthy relationships.	1 2 3 4
25	Physical Security	Knowledge that your spouse will take care of you, protect you and provide for your basic needs.	1 2 3 4
26	Priorities, Family	Establishing general priorities for marriage, family and self, are important. All of these priorities should be discussed with your partner so that you can mutually identify how these priorities can be worked and whether or not they are realistic.	1 2 3 4
27	Respect	To treat people in the manner in which you expect to be treated. To show consideration for another person. Acknowledgement, appreciation, recognition and consideration of another person's beliefs, knowledge, advice, etc. Verbal and non-verbal communication demonstrating that you value the other person.	1 2 3 4
28	Roles and Expectations	You have established roles in your relationship along with specific expectations for each person's responsibilities.	1 2 3 4
29	Romance	Romance usually implies some sort of expression of your strong romantic love for your partner. This includes a deep desire to connect with him/her intimately and is followed up by an effort to find creative ways in which you can express how much you appreciate and value your partner. Cards, flowers, going out to dinner, verbally sharing your love, etc. are all examples of being romantic.	1 2 3 4
30	Sexuality and Sexual Affection	Touching, hugs, caressing, etc. that are intended to be sexual teasers or foreplay techniques. This type of affection is used to help get your partner interested or ready for sexual activity that might lead to sexual intercourse, or other preferred methods of stimulation.	1 2 3 4
31	Spiritual Unity	Having a shared spiritual life is important to many couples. When so, each person in the relationship has certain spiritual expectations for the other. Defining what that is becomes important in the relationship.	1 2 3 4
32	Trust	Knowing that the other person will take care not to expose your weaknesses in a critical way. Once weaknesses are known, it is important that your partner not use them to hurt you in any way. This includes being open, honest, holding no secrets between each other. Emotional and physical affairs are the greatest breaches of trust.	1 2 3 4
33			1 2 3 4
34			1 2 3 4
35			1 2 3 4

TWO CYCLES IN RELATIONSHIPS

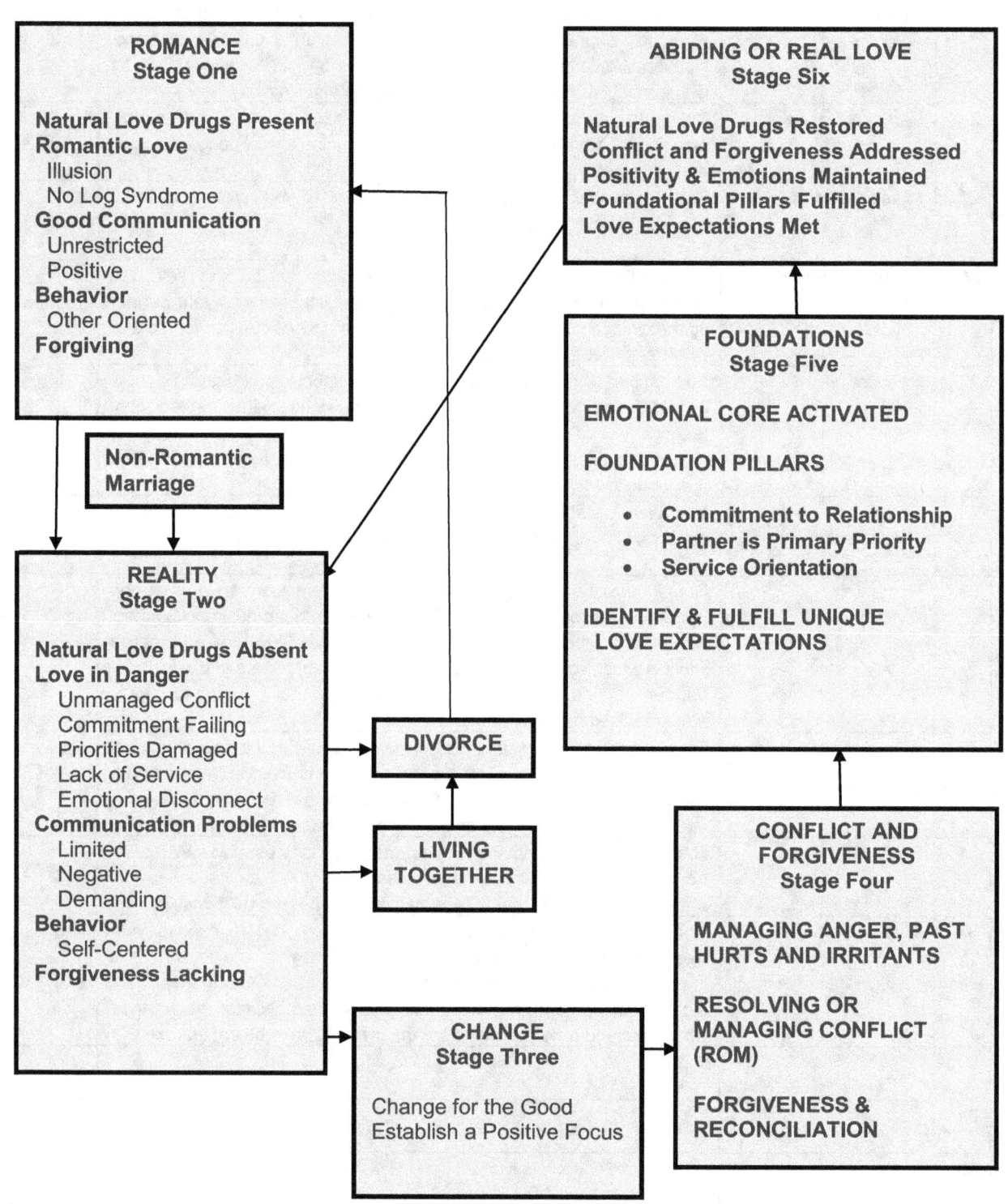

ROMANCE
Stage One

Natural Love Drugs Present
Romantic Love
  Illusion
  No Log Syndrome
Good Communication
  Unrestricted
  Positive
Behavior
  Other Oriented
Forgiving

Non-Romantic Marriage

REALITY
Stage Two

Natural Love Drugs Absent
Love in Danger
  Unmanaged Conflict
  Commitment Failing
  Priorities Damaged
  Lack of Service
  Emotional Disconnect
Communication Problems
  Limited
  Negative
  Demanding
Behavior
  Self-Centered
Forgiveness Lacking

DIVORCE

LIVING TOGETHER

CHANGE
Stage Three

Change for the Good
Establish a Positive Focus

ABIDING OR REAL LOVE
Stage Six

Natural Love Drugs Restored
Conflict and Forgiveness Addressed
Positivity & Emotions Maintained
Foundational Pillars Fulfilled
Love Expectations Met

FOUNDATIONS
Stage Five

EMOTIONAL CORE ACTIVATED

FOUNDATION PILLARS

  • **Commitment to Relationship**
  • **Partner is Primary Priority**
  • **Service Orientation**

IDENTIFY & FULFILL UNIQUE LOVE EXPECTATIONS

CONFLICT AND FORGIVENESS
Stage Four

MANAGING ANGER, PAST HURTS AND IRRITANTS

RESOLVING OR MANAGING CONFLICT (ROM)

FORGIVENESS & RECONCILIATION

Willingness to Change and a Positive Focus

Step One

CHANGE FOR THE GOOD
Handout

Look in the mirror. Really, look in the mirror. Are you the person you want to be physically, emotionally, behaviorally? Do you really like yourself? If you don't like yourself, or if you don't like certain aspects of yourself, you can be assured that your partner senses that and may very well agree. If you are to have a good relationship with anyone you must start with yourself. However, you should never produce cosmetic or superficial changes just to please your partner or anyone else for that matter. If you legitimately can see that there are parts of you that could improve it's important to accept it. And yes, do something about it.....change. If you are changing for the betterment of yourself then it is change for the good. This change should be for you. It should in some way make you a better person. Good change is change that you produce for yourself. Change that betters you in some way and in turn can better any relationship you are in. For instance:

- If you don't like the weight you are at, change it both for your health sake and in order to look better in the mirror for yourself.
- If you don't like the way your hair looks, change it so that that you can be the best you can be and in turn boost your self-image.
- If you don't like the clothes you wear, change them so that you like the way you look which in turn will boost your self-image.
- If you don't like the way you talk with your partner, change it. Say words that are positive and caring even in the worst of times.
- If you don't like that you are negative, change your mind so that you can be a more positive, loving constructive person.
- If you don't like the anger inside of you, you must learn to let it go. Resolve it so that you no longer have to carry something that can come out at most inopportune times.
- If you don't...... You get the picture.

> *At the very least being willing to change for the good can do nothing less than help you grow and become a better version of yourself.*

Change can be good especially when that change causes you to feel better about yourself. Sometimes you may get feedback from others regarding small parts of you that may need to change. Value those bits of information. It your friends or partner is right, and you can see that it would make you a better person if you changed make the change. However, to change you must be willing. Without willingness, even if you obtain information that could help you be a better person in even a small way, it may not happen. You have to be willing to change for the good. If change for the good it to occur there are two things that can help make that happen.

- Willingness to Change
- Establish a Positive Focus

Willingness to Change

Willingness is the key that opens the door to any kind of change. When in conflict most people will say, "I am who I am and so don't try to change me." Some people actually say that they won't change even though their relationship might be on the line. Often such a statement is made when the person is frustrated, feels pressured, angry, etc. Regardless, the truth of the matter is that we all change. Education produces change. Work produces change. Relationships produce change. As we involve ourselves with other people or situations it quickly becomes evident that we must adapt. We learn that if we are to keep a job, we do what our boss expects. If we want to graduate from school or finish a training program we must learn and be able to utilize our newfound knowledge. If we don't learn, grow and change it becomes painfully obvious that our job, our relationship and often this world quickly outpaces us. We become less effective, less useful, less needed and lose out on things that we would love to maintain in our lives. So, because we are intelligent, thoughtful people we change. We learn. We grow and become better for it. This by no means suggests that we change our personality or who we are as a person. This simply suggests that we must have an open mindedness to alter some smaller things that can make us a better person. A person who will have a better marriage relationship.

Let's look at this in another way. Assume that you know a man who has been with his partner for a few years. In that time his partner has:

- lovingly dissuaded him from making very poor decisions
- helped him develop greater self-confidence
- aided in reducing his insecurities
- helped him feel more secure about his 'manliness'
- encouraged him to be more assertive in dealing with people who have traditionally taken advantage of him
- taught him what she needed romantically
- helped him see the value of honest, open communication
- encouraged and supported him in becoming a non-smoker for health reasons
- helped him see how much better life is when he is fiscally responsible
- encouraged him to become the best he could be in bowling because even though it was difficulty to do well he loved it

As a result, the man changed significantly and wasn't upset about it at all. Everything he changed helped him be a better, more capable person. He is now a better model of himself than he was before he changed with her help and encouragement.

This is not suggesting that you change your personality or who you are deep down. However, we are talking about improving the overall package. We all should welcome help, advice, etc. from others that can actually change us for the better. We are not being forced to change. However, we are being shown how we can improve ourselves. We are being shown possibilities and the advantages they offer if we make adjustments in our lives that will usually make us better. Regardless, we still have the option of simply not listening.

With this in mind you should want to try new things, or do things in different ways at times. You should want to find out how you can adjust for your partner so that you can accommodate him in ways that make him feel more loved. You should explore how you can be a better person simply by considering your words before you speak. Taking time to be more considerate in your words will not cause you to 'lose' yourself. To the contrary you will enhance who you are and how you interact with the world around you in a positive way. You will grow. You will change. It is also important that you explore how you can be a better husband or wife by learning what your partner wants, needs and desires. You should seek to be selfless in your relationship so that you can put your partner first and make your relationship something truly special. All of these things are good. They produce positive growth. Life cannot be stagnant. It requires change if it is to grow and be healthy. Anyone who is not willing to change sets himself and his partner up for pain and frustration.

So, how do you go about identifying what needs to be changed? Who in your life will be gently honest with you so that you can see what you could do to grow, to become a better version of yourself? It could be a friend, or a therapist, but when possible it should be your partner. You both should desire to help each other grow, because when you do you both benefit from it. Your lives together should be a work in progress. You should be sharpening each other to become all that you can be. Regardless, if you don't have the courage or desire to seek your partner's feedback regarding your relationship you cannot sharpen each other. In such a circumstance your relationship may very well stagnate and eventually die. So, in summary you must be able to do the following:

1   You must be open to change. You must see that change is not only possible but essential for your personal growth and relationship health.
2   You must be willing to listen to others, and/or look within yourself to see what kind of change needs to happen. Be open minded. Consider what others say that might suggest as a weakness. What could you do to address each issue in order to become a better person?
3   You must be willing to make the changes if you are to grow and become a better version of yourself. Talk to your partner regarding his/her perspective on how you could grow in any identified area. Once identified, determine what you can do to produce positive change and growth.
4   You must take the first step in change by being more positive and less negative. In doing so you may very well produce tremendous change in your partner.

Here are some characteristics that can be seen if you are is willing to change for the better in a relationship.

- You listen to your partner and actively seek to understand what you are doing that may be causing difficulties.
- When you hear how your behavior, attitudes, etc. are causing problems in the relationship you are open to exploring new behaviors, attitudes, etc.
- As you look at conflict in your relationship you first evaluate what your role is in the conflict, and determine what you can do differently to make things better.
- You admit that when you look at the negative it simply can activate your own negativity. So, you commit to focusing on the positive traits, behaviors, etc. of your partner.
- You choose to take your time before you speak in order to choose words that are helpful rather than hurtful.
- Be willing to listen to others about your strengths and weaknesses and discuss how you can change in ways that will improve who you are and how you relate to your partner.
- Willingness to change isn't about changing your personality. It's about being positive about being open to trying new things, thinking about how you can be more loving in your word choices, how you can be more selfless and less selfish in your life.
- You should want to find out how you can adjust for your partner so that you can accommodate him/her in ways that make him/her feel more loved.
- You should seek to be selfless in your relationship so that you can put your partner first and make your relationship something truly special.
- You should welcome help and advice from others that can actually help you see what you can do to change for the better.

NOTE: Willingness to change in a relationship is a two-way street. It is an extremely rare occurrence for only one person in the relationship to need to change or grow so that the relationship can be what it needs to be. So, ask the question, "What can I do to change in order to make me the best person I can be. If I do that, won't it also give our relationship a chance to become the best it can be?" Now, it's your choice. Are you willing to change both for your personal benefit and for the benefit of your relationship? If you are, you will see many positive benefits both for yourself and your partner.

What You Are Willing to Change
Couple Worksheet

Name:_____ **Date:**_____

Instructions:
Read each of the statements below and determine if there are any other things you want either one of you to consider changing. List three or more if desired.

1.

2.

3.

Add any area of change to be considered in the boxes below.   When finished read each of the areas of change together and check if you would be willing to change in that area.

Wife		Areas of Change	Husband	
Yes	No		Yes	No
		Are you willing to change your appearance?		
		Are you willing to change who you are as a person....your personality?		
		Are you willing to change how you dress?		
		Are you willing to be committed to your relationship?		
		Are you willing to change your hairstyle?		
		Are you willing to change the things you enjoy doing?		
		Are you willing to change your political views?		
		Are you willing to quit smoking?		
		Are you willing to learn better manners?		
		Are you willing to make your partner your first priority?		
		Are you willing to change your appearance?		
		Are you willing to change your hobbies?		
		Are you willing to change your job?		
		Are you willing to meet your partner's love expectations?		
		Are you willing to change your social circle?		
		Are you willing to change your church home?		
		Are you willing to change how you handle money?		
		Are you willing to be service oriented in your relationship?		
		Are you willing to change your religious views, beliefs, or values?		
		Are you willing to get rid of bad habits or behaviors that harm you or your relationship?		
		Are you willing to change where you live?		
		Are you willing to focus on positives instead of negatives?		
		Are you willing to help your partner grow by offering kind suggestions?		
		Are you willing to let go of negative reactions to what your partner says or does?		

What You Are Willing to Change
Individual Worksheet

Name:_____ **Date:**_____

Instructions:

Look at the 'What Are You Willing to Change' worksheet and for any changes you are willing to make:

1. State the specific thing you are willing to change
2. State the reason you are willing to make that change
3. Identify the date you will commit to begin the change.

I am willing to make this change:	Reason	I commit to begin this by this date:

Establish a Positive Focus
Handout

Research has shown that when people are positive toward one another it produces a positive chemical change in their systems that make them feel closer. With this in mind anything we can do to promote positivity is a plus in a relationship. For our purposes we are going to look at three ways that you can increase a positive focus in your life and in the lives of those around you. It's up to you to identify how you can make each of these more of a reality in your daily life. The more it becomes part of your life, the more positive you will be. It will also provide motivation for you to make your relationship the best it can be. The three ways you can be more positive are:

- Positively Change Your Inner Self
- Be Positive Toward Self
- Be Positive Toward your Partner or Others

Positively Change Your Inner Self

For your own health and overall benefit you must learn to develop a positive sense of self. You should learn how to change yourself from the inside out. James Allen wrote a very short but powerful book called, As a Man Thinketh in 1903. The primary thought found in the book was based on a scripture found in Proverbs 23:7 (KJV) that stated, 'As a man thinks in his heart, so he becomes'. Maxwell Maltz in his amazing book entitled Psycho Cybernetics (1960) stated that what a man thinks he becomes. The advent of Cognitive Behavior Therapy also seemed to take root in the early 1960's and was officially 'born'. However, when the study of irrational thoughts by Ellis (1977) and the cognitive schemata of mental illness by Beck (1993) took root Cognitive Behavioral Psychology was well on its way to becoming a dominant force in therapy. We learned that what was in our mind actually prompted us to speak or act out what we were thinking. So, what you think, you say. What you think and say, you ultimately do. What you think actually determines how you respond to life's situations. Ultimately what you think determines who you are becoming on a day by day minute by minute basis. With this in mind it is easy to see how important thinking is in your personal health and in the health of your relationship.

The first thing you can do is reprogram your inner mind to be more positive just as Coue, Allen, Maltz and others have suggested. Here are two methods that might help accomplish this.

- As a Man Thinketh
- MGR Goal Vision

> *A man is literally what he thinks, his character being the complete sum of all his thoughts (Allen, 1903).*

Be Positive Toward Self

The second thing you can work on is learn to be more positive for yourself. Sometimes that means 'fixing' some things. Other times it simply means that you learn how to be the best you can be and enjoy it. How can you be more positive in nature? Many of these supplemental strategies may be found in the Marriage Go Round Therapist Manuals.

- Establish a Positive Focus Handout
- As a Man Thinketh Handout and Strategy
- Marriage Go Round Goal Vision Worksheet and Exercise
- Become the Best You Can Be Individual Worksheet
- My Personal Positives Individual Worksheet
- Self-Image Model
- Self-Image Evaluation
- Self-Image, Historical Issues and Your Partner Individual Worksheet

Be Positive Toward your Partner or Others

Third, identify how you can exhibit a positive focus toward your partner or others. One of the greatest changes you can make if you are to have a healthy, vibrant, exciting married life it simply to focus on those things that are positive regarding your partner. You have to look for positives and remove the negatives. Look for things your partner does that is positive and briefly comment on them. Look for character traits you love to see in your partner and let your partner know how valuable those traits are to you. Here are some ways you can do this on a day-by-day basis. Many of these supplemental strategies may be found in the Marriage Go Round Therapist Manuals.

- The Great Pretender Worksheet and Exercise
- Become a Positive Spouse Worksheet and Exercise
- Maximize Your Positives Toward Your Partner Worksheet
- The One Week Challenge Worksheet
- Looking Into The Mirror Worksheet
- Rules for Positive Partnering Handout

As a Man Thinketh
Handout and Strategy

"As a man thinks in his heart, so he becomes." (Proverbs 23:7 KJV)

What you think you become. The good thing is that you can choose what you think. You can change what you 'naturally' think on a day by day basis by simply changing what you feed your mind daily. You can be positive instead of negative. You can look for the best in your partner instead of the worst. To explain this we need to go back in history a bit and look at the work of a man called Emile Coue. Emile (1857-1926), a physician and French Druggist formulated the Laws of Suggestion. He is also known for encouraging his patients to say to themselves 20-30 times each night before going to sleep, "Every day in every way, I am getting better and better".

Basically, Coué emphasized the role of positive thinking in self-improvement. Through this he proposed bridging the gap between behavior and cognition in order for the individual to be successful in achieving something he or she wanted. One amazing thing he found as a result of his research was that by reciting a mantra that involved positive thoughts, it actually improved the chance that someone will achieve a goal or objective.

Coué also suggested that any idea exclusively occupying the mind eventually turns into reality as long as it is within the realm of possibility. For instance, if a person has lost an arm or leg in an accident their body/mind cannot make the body part grow back. However, if a person believes that anxiety, depression, etc. is disappearing, then it may very well be reduced or go away. On the negative side if the person thinks that he is anxious, depressed, etc. his body and mind will accept this as truth and attempt to make it happen. Coué realized that it is extremely important to focus on and imagine the desired positive results, because the mind will attempt to accomplish what it sees or hears. Years later James Allen wrote a powerful little book entitled, As a Man Thinketh. In this book he stated, *"They themselves are makers of themselves by virtue of the thoughts which they choose and encourage; that mind is the master-weaver, both of the inner garment of character and the outer garment of circumstance, and that, as they may have hitherto woven in ignorance and pain they may now weave in enlightenment and happiness."* Allen continues by saying, *"A man is literally what he thinks, his character being the complete sum of all his thoughts. As the plant springs from, and could not be without the seed, so every act of a man springs from the hidden seeds of thought, and could not have appeared without them. This applies equally to those acts called 'spontaneous' and 'unpremeditated' as to those which are deliberately executed."* What Allen suggested in this powerful book goes right along with what Coue had been saying for years.

Now let's go back to Coue for a moment. Considering all this information Coue determined that the subconscious mind is entirely reprogrammable. For it to be programmed or reprogrammed you simply put into your mind the images or statements that you want your mind to internalize and work toward. This is why he encouraged his patients to say to themselves 20-30 times each night before going to sleep, "Every day in every way, I am getting better and better". This is also why he encouraged his patients to imagine or say the kind of things that would focus on the desired outcome. Basically he wanted these images or statements to be internalized by the unconscious mind. Why? Coue's forth psychological standard says, 'WHEN IMAGINATION AND THE WILL (conscious mind) ARE IN FIGHT, IT IS ALWAYS THE IMAGINATION WHICH CARRIES IT, WITHOUT ANY EXCEPTION.'

This is extremely interesting and appears to be sound information. Before we start applying this concept to marriage issues, let's jump forward about thirty years after Coue published his findings. In 1960 Maxwell Maltz, M.D., F.I.C.S. wrote a book that has sold more than 3 million copies. It was entitled, <u>Psycho-Cybernetics: A New Technique for Using your Subconscious Power</u>. Maltz took information from Coue and from Dr. Norbert Weiner and applied it to self-image and overall success. Dr. Weiner was a brilliant mathematician and a key player who worked on guided missile technology during World War II. This technology played a key role in the development of Maltz's work.

Maltz stated that, "Cybernetics regards the human brain, nervous system, and muscular system, as a highly complex servo-mechanism. It is an automatic goal-seeking machine which 'steers' its way to a target or goal by use of feed-back data and stored information, automatically correcting course when necessary" (Maltz 1960). Basically, he believed that your mind has a servo-mechanism inside of it that is goal-striving in nature. It is both impersonal and automatic. Simply stated, its goal is to give you what you are asking for. Your mind determines what you want as it receives images, thoughts, and words that you feed it. As soon as these messages are processed by the mind it seeks to make happen what it has internalized. Just as with Coue, Maltz believes that this device is much more powerful than human will.

We are close to putting this all together so hang on for a bit. Maltz also suggested that it is the job of the conscious mind to decide what you want….to select the goals you want to achieve and to spend time concentrating on what you want. To focus on what you do not want will produce unwanted results. So, we are to focus on what we want, not what we don't want. So, assuming that there is a part of you that wants to be positive and constructive when you are around your partner, what can you send your mind that will make it hard for you to accomplish this? First, you may send your mind active statements or see images that are exactly what you don't want. You may say "I mostly have negative feelings about my partner. He just frustrates me so much." Such an active negative statement or image that will tell this servo-mechanism or goal seeking device to find a place and time where you can be negative toward your partner. You can be assured that times and places will be found if this occurs. There are also passive negative statements that cause this servo-mechanism to actively seek out what you don't want. For instance, "I want to stop being negative toward my partner." Or, "I need to be less negative toward my partner." These seem to be positive statements, but the focus is on what you don't want to do, not what you want to do. You keep sending your mind or goal seeking device the image of negativity, arguing, anger, etc. and it continues to seek out opportunities. We often share this scenario. A gentleman has worked hard all day at not being negative. He has told himself he can go a day without being negative. He has listened to others being negative, but has worked through it. He is proud that he makes it to the end of work. Now he has to drive home. When he first meets his wife she says, 'I thought you would call me before you left. Dinner won't be ready for a while. I've told you over and over if you just let me know it would make things easier for both of us." The next thing out of his mouth is usually a negative reaction to his wife. His unconscious mind or his goal seeking device is trying to find a way to be negative. It is seeking to find what he has been thinking about. So you can see to think that you don't want to be negative, can be as bad as thinking that you actually want to be negative when it comes to your goal seeking device. You must think what you want so that your unconscious mind can actually help produce positive results.

So, to sum up it is important to only send your mind (goal seeking device) a positive message that says what you want to happen. Instead of saying you are going to stop being negative, you will say I want to be positive in what I think and say. You need to envision yourself as a person who is positive. You need to see yourself saying positive, constructive things when you are with your partner. There is a tool you can use to help you accomplish this. It is called, Marriage Go Round Goal Vision. This technique can be used to change any unhealthy part of you if you take time to use it. When used this technique will help you reprogram your unconscious mind and the goal-seeking servo-mechanism within it to do all that it can to help you become what you want to be for yourself and in your relationship.

In addition, you can choose to say a mantra to yourself that suggests you want to be positive. You need to say your mantra about being positive daily.

Example: "I am committed to loving my partner and to be positive and constructive every minute, every hour, every day for the rest of my life."

Every time you envision your Goal Vision....every time you say your mantra you are reprogramming your unconscious mind and the goal-seeking servo-mechanism within it to do all that it can to help you become a positive, constructive person. What is your mantra? Take a moment and think exactly what you want it to say before writing it below. Say this mantra to yourself in the morning, periodically during the day, and in the evening before you go to bed. You may also want to say it every time your partner does something that triggers negativity inside of you. Take control. Teach your mind what you want to be and make it happen.

Personal Mantra

Marriage Go Round

Chart & Overview

**Secondary
Love Expectations
Addressed**
Identify and Address
Level 3 and 4 Issues

Identify and Fulfill Primary Love Expectations
Identify and Address Level 2 Issues

**Commitment to
Relationship**
Level One Core Issue

Partner as Primary Priority
Level One Core Issue

Becoming Service Oriented
Level One Core Issue

Three Foundational Pillars
Address Level One Core Issues

Positive Emotions Activated
Foundational Core Issue

Conflict and Forgiveness
Cooling Down the Crisis

Manage Anger, Past Hurts and Irritants

Step Two

Self-Regulation, Anger and Conflict
Handout and Worksheet

Self-regulation is often a term used when dealing with ADHD issues. However, it also applies to all of us in regard to how well we control our emotions, our words or our actions in regards to our partner. In 1988 Fincham and Bradbury finalized research that suggested whatever judgments you tend to make regarding why your partner either says or does something impacts how you will respond. In other words, your judgments can lead you to perceiving negative when negative is not there. When you throw negativity on top of perceived negativity it often only makes things worse. It's important that we learn self-control and think about or verify what we are perceiving before we get upset and react. Another way of saying this is, 'Make sure you actually disagree before you argue or get mad about disagreeing.' If you simply utilize self-control long enough to verify if your partner means what you think he means you may end up disagreeing much less and possibly have far fewer reasons to be angry. Consider using the 'Verification Challenge' strategy found in the MGR Second Journey to help with this issue. To help address this problem please respond to the following statements or questions.

Give some specific examples as to how your lack of self-control caused problems for you in your relationship.

Look back at each of these examples and write down how your lack of control damaged your relationship in each instance.

What can you do physically to help get yourself back in control of yourself, e.g., call a time out, get a glass of water, sit down, count to ten. List a few things that you would be willing to try.

Time Outs for Marriage
Handout

Have you ever tried to resolve or manage conflict when one or both parties are emotionally upset? If you have, you know that it doesn't work. When feelings get in the way solutions for conflict are next to impossible to identify. That's why it is important to take time outs when either person seems to be getting upset. If you don't, it will probably only get worse. So, here are some pointers that may help you with developing a time out that will work for the two of you.

Why Time Outs Don't Always Work

In theory taking a time out as a way to help resolve conflict in marriage is a great idea. However, unless both parties take a "proper" time out, it's not going to be an effective conflict resolution tool for the couple. There are a few reasons why "time outs" may not work for a couple:

- The time away is spent ruminating on negative emotions rather than focusing on the core issue
- One or both parties may take a "time out" simply to escape the issue
- One or both parties may be looking for a way to distract themselves from the pressing problem at hand and use it as a way to move on without addressing the issue

If either individual spent the time apart focusing on any one of the above three items, once the couple resumes their previous discussion, they would most assuredly end up right back where they were before they parted for the time out because their outlook or perspective hasn't really changed. In fact, an individual may feel even more fueled up and ready to argue rather than seek resolution.

Things to Avoid

- Following the person who requested a time-out. This inevitably leads to an escalation of conflict. Respect each other's need to get away, but always establish a time to come back so that you can continue your conversation.
- Storming away. If you leave showing how upset you are without explaining why you are leaving, where you are going and if you are coming back or not you simply magnify the problem
- Time-outs done when either of you are not ready. If either of you are overtired, or under excessive stress it may be best to wait.
- Avoid communicating in an angry tone of voice as you leave for your time out. For instance, "You make me so mad," or "I can't talk to you."

Agree that Times-Outs are Good and Should Be Used

It is important that the couple establish a mutual understanding that time-outs are not just okay, but important and helpful. Make sure that there is an agreement regarding the use of the time out before you find yourselves in an escalating argument. For example, you could both agree on:

1. When a Time-Out should be used
2. The positive reasons for a time out, which is to change your state of mind, to create space and time to self-soothe and reflect on what to do next, and not to avoid or control the argument,
3. How a time-out could be carried out.

Understanding the Need and Timing of a Time-Out

The best time for a couple to take a time-out is when there is a shift in the internal state of one or both parties that will put them at the risk of escalating the conversation into an unnecessary or damaging argument. When the conversation is at this critical point, both individuals are at a higher risk of saying something they would regret. This is one of the most important reasons why a time-out should be used.

The Purpose of a Time Out

A time-out is never a permanent solution for how to resolve or manage conflict in in any relationship. Time-out should be considered a temporary measure that the couple uses to return to a healthier, more positive, constructive frame of mind so that they can address issues.

What You Should Be doing During a Time-Out

Simply being apart is not the most constructive thing that occurs. It does give you some time to calm down and think, but simply being apart will not lead to resolution or compromise. It takes more than that. There are a number of things each person should be considering while they are in their time out. For instance:

1. Take time to de-stress. Walk, read a book, work out or do anything that helps you calm down.
2. Think about why you are angry or upset. What is really your underlying motivation for getting so upset? Could it be hurt, fear, sadness? Think about your underlying feelings and how you could share them in a more positive way with your partner
3. Consider how you are responsible for any part of the conflict or problem.
4. Think about the words you are using, your tone of voice, and body language.
5. Are you doing anything that makes it more difficult to rationally discuss the issue?
6. Are your words or actions making it difficult for your partner to listen and accept what you are saying?
7. Is there a solution in the middle that you could suggest that might make it better for both of you instead of being in a win-lose situation?
8. Is there anything you need to change that would make anything regarding this situation better?
9. Do you need to repair any damage before you begin your discussion again? If so, when you return do your best to repair any damage that may have been done.

If you identify anything insightful, as you ponder the above, consider how you will communicate it to your partner and how it impacts the current situation. If it causes you to change your stance, explain it to your partner.

Rules for a Constructive Time-Out

If a time-out is to be effective it must follow clearly defined procedures that both partners agree to. Not following these rules or procedures can put the relationship at risk.

1. Have a specific way that each of you can call for a time out.
2. Reassure your partner that you are not giving up on the discussion and that you fully intend on returning so that you can continue your discussion.
3. State how long you need to be gone (no less than 30 minutes and no more than 24 hours).
4. Give each other space so that you can review what you should be doing during the time out (See What You Should Be doing During a Time-Out).
5. Return and take time to heal. Apologize if necessary and reaffirm your love and desire to heal.
6. Share what you have learned from your timeout before beginning any kind of resolution or management of the issue.
7. Continue to discuss options to resolve or manage the conflict in a better way for both of you.

NOTE: Use any of the strategies found in this manual or from other resources to help you as you seek to work through the issue.

Although it is not optimal, sometimes it is better to 'sleep on it' so that you can look at things fresh the next day.   Sometimes when you give something time and do some introspection you realize that the issue was not as important as it seemed to be the day before.

Resolve or Manage Conflict (ROM)

Step Three

> *"Conflict can either be a purifying fire, or a consuming flame."*

The Underlying Key to Conflict Management
Handout

Conflict is inevitable in all relationships. It is also inevitable that you will not resolve or compromise some of your conflicts. It is important to either resolve or compromise as much as is possible, but reality raises its ugly head and periodically keeps us from doing either at times. So when this happens, or even before it happens how must you be prepared to get through these times without damaging your relationship? Let's take a minute and discuss this.

Emotions are what Hold Us Together

From the very beginning of your relationship feelings or emotions are what eventually drew you together as a couple. These emotions are essential in an ongoing love relationship. Without them your relationship will gradually die away. So, if they are so important we should be making it a priority to maintain our 'love' feelings for our partner.

Before you deal with conflict you should be doing all that you can to enhance the positive emotions that you have for each other. For instance:

- Having fun
- Hugging
- Kissing
- Being Romantic
- Doing exciting things together
- Doing new things together
- Exercising together

If you aren't doing any of the above things on a consistent basis you are probably distancing emotionally.

Guidelines for Dealing with Conflict
Handout

1. Set the right atmosphere. This can occur when you do the following:

   - Take the phone off the hook.
   - Get the kids in bed or at a friend's house.
   - Shut the front door (make the house look deserted from the outside).
   - Choose a neutral location if it is not at home.
   - Schedule enough time to come to a resolution.

2. Work on conflict by appointment only. Always make sure that your partner has a say in when you will sit down to attempt resolution.

3. Discuss only one topic at a time. Make sure it is resolved before you discuss any other topic. Set a time limit of fifteen to thirty minutes maximum.

4. Don't try to win. If one partner wins, the couple loses.

5. Define the topic to be discussed. Both should agree on the definition.

6. Keep to the here and now (don't bring up the past).

7. Focus on the problem, not your partner (do not attack your partner's character).

8. Do not counter attack if your partner attacks you (stay in your adult rational mode).

9. Call foul when your partner breaks a rule or attacks you.

10. Have as a goal, the desire to come to a mutually acceptable decision.

11. If you find yourself tensing up take a "time out" and relax a little. Don't let yourself get bent out of shape to the point that you can't discuss things rationally.

12. Be honest and straightforward. Don't play mental games with your partner such as:

    - Martyrdom
    - Mind Reading
    - Sarcasm
    - Exaggeration
    - Minimization

13. Don't leave mentally or physically until both parties feel like the problem has been resolved or should be tabled for an agreed upon time (see time out).

Forgive and Reconcile

Step Four

Forgiveness and Reconciliation
Handout

Forgiveness: Forgiveness is not so much for the offender as it is for the offended. It is unhealthy to harbor bitterness, anger, resentment, etc. It is important to forgive, but it is also important to remember and learn from any such event. Learning to protect ourselves from future hurts can be minimized if we learn how to watch for situations where we might indeed be hurt. Learning to set healthy boundaries for future situations is essential.

Examples of How We Can Hurt Our Partner

- Wife/husband who is physically abused

- Emotional or Verbal Abuse

- Affairs

- Money is misused, e.g., control issue, damaging credibility, hurting the family

- Dishonesty has hurt relationship

- Lack of emotional connection

- Anger

- No personal space

Roles of the Offended and the Offender

Offended	Offender
I can immediately, unconditionally, and continually forgive someone who has hurt me.	If I have hurt another person, I need to ask for forgiveness, and seek to make restitution in order to express my desire for reconciliation.
However.....	However.....
I may not always be able to effect a Reconciliation with the offender.	I am in no position to demand it.

NOTE: The offended person, not the offender, holds all the cards! However, in a relationship you should make an attempt to make things right so that you can begin to heal the relationship.

> *Forgiveness depends upon me;*
> *reconciliation depends upon us.*

Necessary Ingredients for Reconciliation

Forgiveness without a Request for Forgiveness:

- The offended needs to forgive regardless if the other person requests it.
- However, without a request for forgiveness there will be no true reconciliation.
- Nor will the offended be able to trust or the offender be able to rebuild trust!

Forgiveness with a Request for Forgiveness:

- The offended needs to forgive regardless if the other person requests it.
- The offender must say, "I'm sorry" in a way that shows (s)he means it.
- However, requesting forgiveness alone does not mean that you can reconcile.
- Requesting forgiveness does not automatically rebuild trust!

Restitution:

- The offender begins with an attempt to demonstrate genuine sorrow to the person he has wronged by saying, "I'm sorry".
- The offender communicates a desire to provide restitution in order to make up for the damage done.
- Restitution validates the sincerity of our sorrow and helps the offended party to begin to heal.
- When restitution is offered and given, it becomes a pathway to rebuild trust.
- Trust is 'slowly' rebuilt as the offender commits acts of being trustworthy. Sometimes this must start with small things. This often requires a greater amount of trust building than is normal due to the fact that trust has been seriously damaged.
- Ways of trust building should be identified by the offended and communicated to the offender.

However:

- If restitution is attempted without genuine sorrow that is evidenced by a change in behavior and a desire to utilize the trust building behaviors that will help heal the offended, it is often not successful.
- Healing of the pain and damage needed for reconciliation doesn't happen instantaneously...it takes time. It cannot be hurried, i.e., "I said I'm sorry, so get over it."
- For some this time of healing or rehabilitation requires the assistance of other people (counseling).

Reconciliation:

- Reconciliation gradually occurs as trust is rebuilt and as long as the person is not offended again.
- Sometimes the pain is so great and/or trust is damaged so often that reconciliation becomes difficult or impossible for the offended.

Forgiveness Defined
Handout

Forgiveness: .	Forgiveness occurs when you grant a pardon to someone, and cease to blame or feel resentment about an offense or the offender.

Forgiveness Isn't	Forgiveness Is
Natural It is more natural for us to fight back, to take justice into our own hands.	**An act of love** True forgiveness is to want the best for the other person.
Without Cost Giving trust back unconditionally. It has been damaged and must gradually be developed again.	**Powerful** When forgiveness is given it produces healing and freedom from resentment, hostility and anger.
Indifference Forgiveness is not inaction or indifference. Forgetting when you haven't dealt with a problem can bring no peace.	**An Act of the Will** You do not have to feel like it to forgive. It is and should be more an act of will than feeling. It is a decision!
Agreeing With the Wrong Forgiveness is not agreeing with the wrong.	

Activate Your Emotional Core

Step Five

Emotional Reconnection and Bonding
Handout

Before you reconnect emotionally it is important that each person work at making sure that you are not using destructive or harmful language or actions. Consider maximizing your positive communication with your partner and you will see benefits immediately. Each of the strategies mentioned below are meant to be used to help the couple reconnect with lost positive feelings they have had for each other. Sometimes it is hard to get a couple to engage in therapy when they are so convinced that all they have is pain and frustration with each other. Therapeutically, these strategies help reset each person's brain so that it will think more positively about his or her partner which gives them and the therapist a better chance to produce long lasting positive change. Cognitive Behavior Therapy suggests that if you change a negative thought into the positive opposite, it can have a major impact on the individual's mental health or perspective. Maxwell Maltz in his classic book entitled, Psycho-Cybernetics stated that if you imagine something it has a much better chance of becoming reality. Émile Coué de la Châtaigneraie was a French psychologist and pharmacist who introduced a popular method of psychotherapy and self-improvement based on optimistic autosuggestion. He stated that when the will and the imagination come into conflict the imagination inevitably wins. He also coined the autosuggestion that has been made popular by Norman Vincent Peale, Robert H. Schuller, and W. Clement Stone. That suggestion was, "Every day, in every way, I'm getting better and better." Émile Coué's underlying belief was that if you think enough about something it will be imprinted on the mind and will have a greater chance of occurring in everyday life. So if all of these similar beliefs or systems are true it behooves us to find a way 'reprogram' our minds so that we can think in a more positive, kindly, loving way toward each other. Here are a number of ways you can reprogram your minds and reconnect emotionally. Many of these supplemental strategies may be found in the Marriage Go Round Therapist Manuals.

- Memories of How You Met
- Memories
- Pictures of Past Love
- Love Sight: Visualization of Love Desired
- Auto suggestion for Love
- Resurrection
- Feelings and Your Relationship Exercise
- Emotional Bonding Handout
- Getting to Know You Game

Emotional Bonding
Handout

Emotional bonding is one of the most important aspects in a relationship. Without this bonding a couple will gradually distance from each other until they no longer have feelings of love for each other. When we first meet someone we go out of our way to spend time with them. We have fun, are romantic, do little things that make them feel special and in general focus on the positive instead of the negative. This promotes a tremendous amount of positive emotional energy. The easy part is that we are often infused with dopamine when we are initially in a new relationship. We have lots of energy, are extremely happy and feel wonderful. In time this seems to wear off. The good news is that you can jump start the dopamine infusion if you work at it. So, two things must occur to build emotional bonding. First, you must experience fun or share interests with each other that make you laugh or enjoy being with each other. This can produce dopamine which enhances your feelings toward your partner. Second, you should make time for romance. Find ways to be romantic with your partner. Being romantic can produce dopamine and also can produce oxytocin which is the love drug in your body. It makes you feel closer to the person you are with. So, your body actually has ways in which it helps you improve your feelings for each other. You just have to take the time to do the things that will trigger the dopamine and oxytocin in your brain. So, if you want to build or rebuild a relationship you must emotionally bond. There are three relatively easy ways in which you can do this.

1. Having Fun
2. Experiencing Common Interests Together (see MGR The Second Journey)
3. Being Romantic

Getting to Know You Game

One fun way of identifying what is fun, romantic or exciting, special to your partner in some way is to have a date and do the, 'Getting To Know You' game. Simply ask the questions on the form assuming you do not know any of that information. Pretend you are on a first or second date and have agreed to 'interview' each other to find out what is important to that person.

Rules for Emotional Bonding on Dates

Times you can have emotional bonding can be ruined if you are not careful or at the very least your time together may not produce the results you want due to small issues. Here are some rules that have been helpful for some couples in the past.

Rule Number One: Never discuss problems on a date! It destroys any bonding or positive emotional energy you may have obtained from your time together.

Rule Number Two: If you want a man to talk, give him something new to talk about. Do something new, fun or exciting.

Rule Number Three: Always eat after having fun or spending time together, not before (you will have more to talk about—make sure you eat at a restaurant that does not have a television)!

Having Fun and Emotional Bonding

Couple Worksheet

Name:_____ Date:_____

Restaurants	Indoor Activities
Rule: To be included on this worksheet the restaurant must be entertaining or extremely unique. It can't just be good food!	An activity that can take place indoors (home or elsewhere) that you believe is fun.

Outdoor Activities	Day Trips, Weekend Vacations
An activity that can take place anyplace outdoors that you believe is fun.	A trip that would provide you with fun activities that both of you would enjoy.

Romance and Emotional Bonding

Couple Worksheet

Your Definition of Romance	
Romance Descriptors:	
Romantic Restaurants	**Romantic Indoor Activities**
Romantic Outdoor Activities	**Romantic Day Trips or Weekend Getaways**

Getting to Know You Game
Couple Exercise and Homework

Service, making your partner a priority, romance and more can only be effective if you know your partner. After they have been married or in relationship for a period of time couples often begin to take for granted that each of them knows what the other wants and likes out of life and specifically the relationship. The problem is that the information is either outdated or has changed. The purpose of this worksheet is to help you get to know your partner all over again.

The name of the person you are getting to know: _____

ASK THE FOLLOWING QUESTIONS!

FOOD

What is your favorite food?

What beverage do you like to drink most often?

What restaurant is your most favorite restaurant?

What are your two most favorite ethnic restaurants?

___Mexican   ___Chinese   ___German   ___Italian   ___Japanese   ___Indian

___American   ___French   ___Other:_____

What is the name of the restaurant and the menu item you would enjoy most at the two ethnic restaurants you chose?

Name of Restaurant: _____ Menu Item:_____

Name of Restaurant: _____ Menu Item:_____

What are your three most favorite home cooked meals?

What is your all time favorite dessert?

VACATION OR GETAWAYS

What type of location would your like most for a vacation?

____ Beach   ___Mountains   ___Other:_____

Would it be: ___more relaxing or   ___where you have a lot of activities

MOVIES

What is your all time favorite movie?

Check the two kinds of movies that you like the most.

___Romantic   ___Comedy   ___Adventure   ___Horror   ___War

___Musicals   ___Science Fiction   ___Romantic Comedy   ___Fantasy

___Other:_____

SPORTS

What are your favorite sports activities that you like to participate in?

What sports do you like to go watch?

FUN

What is your favorite thing to do for fun?

List five things that you like to do that is really fun for you.

    1._____   4._____

    2._____   5._____

    3._____

What is a common interest that you would want to share with your partner (remember, common interests are things that both you enjoy doing or participating in)?

CLOTHES

What is your partner's coat or dress size?

What is your partner's pants or slacks size?

What is your partner's favorite color for clothes?

What is your partner's blouse or shirt size?

HOBBIES

What hobbies do you have that you enjoy?

SEX, ROMANCE AND INTIMACY

What romantic act is most important to you?

How important is sex in your relationship with your partner and what could make it better?

What helps get you into the mood for intimacy and sex the most?

What position(s) do you prefer most when you have sex?

What specific thing can your partner do for you sexually that pleases you the most?

What else would you want your partner to do to make sex more exciting or special for you?

OTHER TOPICS

What is the most important thing your partner can do for you? Be specific!

What kind of flowers or gift do you like the most?

How important is church or spirituality to you?

What kind of music do you like the most?

How could your partner help you better in regards to housework, yard, etc.?

In addition to the area's shown below list any other subjects that come to mind that would be good to discuss if you were wanting to get to know a person.

| . Morals | . Goals | . Children | . Values |
| . Personal Strengths | . Personal Weaknesses | | |

_____   _____

_____   _____

Use the back of the page to write down more information if desired!

NATURAL LOVE DRUGS
THE CHEMISTRY OF RELATIONSHIPS
Handout and Worksheet

Throughout the relationship internal chemistry can play a major role in how a couple builds or fails to build a relationship. This is a handout that generally describes how chemistry can improve the quality of relationship. This chemistry can also help couples renew their relationship if they take the steps needed to insure that their chemistry works in their favor.

Natural Aphrodisiacs

Multiple researchers have identified natural aphrodisiacs that boost desire and closeness in relationships. Dr. Helen Fisher reports that, "Humans have evolved three different brain systems to encourage mating: sex drive (lust), feelings of attachment (trust), and romance (being in love). Each of these systems plays a role in desire, and scientists are now beginning to pinpoint the bodily chemicals that trigger each." She reported that there are specific hormones or chemicals that help produce these relationship responses; Dopamine, Oxytocin and Androgens (Testosterone being the main one).

A Natural Pleasure Enhancer

The first chemical that drives relationships is dopamine, a key player in the brain's pleasure center that's been found to promote romantic love. There are a number of ways that you can increase dopamine in your system which in turn produces a positive euphoria in your relationship. Although once you are past the Romantic Love stage it becomes more difficult to stimulate dopamine in your relationship, it is not impossible. However, it does take some work and your chances improve if you are creative. Some things you can do as a couple are:

- A new activity whether it be fun or romantic
- Try a new food that seems appealing.
- Ride a rollercoaster, go horseback riding, ride a motorcycle or something else that stimulates you.
- The moderate stress of hiking will make the bonding experience better.
- Try something new sexually (position, pretending, meet at hotel, sex outdoors, etc.)
- Do something risky, but not overly dangerous.

Brainstorming

Review the above and then identify things the two of you might do that could possibly increase dopamine levels in your brains.

The Love or Cuddle Hormone

Oxytocin, also known as the "Love or Cuddle" hormone, can produce feelings of trust and attachment. In a study conducted at the University of Zurich, couples who used a nasal spray containing oxytocin before discussing an ongoing marital conflict were more likely to engage in friendly, positive communication than those who didn't take a whiff. When oxytocin is increased by 10-20%, noticeable behavior changes—like feeling more relaxed—result. In addition, oxytocin is a hormone that helps relax and reduce blood pressure and cortisol levels. It increases pain thresholds, has antianxiety effects, and stimulates various types of positive social interaction. In addition, it promotes growth and healing. You can stimulate oxytocin naturally with touch. Some ways you can increase oxytocin in your system are:

- Hold hands
- Trade massages
- Sleep in each other's arms
- Hug
- Really look into your partner's eyes
- Kiss
- Become Sexually Aroused (Plasma oxytocin levels increase during sexual arousal in both women and men)
- Have an Orgasm with your partner (oxytocin is released at a significantly higher level by both men and women at sexual orgasm)
- Watch an emotionally compelling movie (makes oxytocin surge 47%)
- Sing show tunes, or do karaoke if you're doing it with other people
- Partnered dancing. In one experiment, Dr. Zak drew the blood of dancers before and after a night of dancing. He found that the oxytocin levels of the dancers rose 11%, regardless of age or gender.
- Go bungee jumping, rollercoaster riding, or out to see a scary flick. "Doing something thrilling is a great way to connect with somebody,

Brainstorming

As time goes by some couples become less intimate, especially when they are having ongoing unresolved conflict. However, if you want to give yourself a better chance at reconnecting emotionally and possibly intimately you need to experience some oxytocin releasing activities. This also makes you more emotional energy to address conflict that is causing difficulties for your relationship. Review the above and then identify things the two of you might do that could possibly increase oxytocin levels in your brains.

Sex Drive Hormone

Sex drive is associated with a class of hormones called androgens. The specific androgen is testosterone. Yes, women have it too. Whether you be a man or a women if you don't have enough of it your sex drive can do down. There are a number of ways that you can increase testosterone in your system which in turn stimulates your sex drive. They are:

- Get a prescription for testosterone
- Play competitive sports (women seem to get a bigger boost than men prior to a competition)
- Studies suggest that making love can also raise testosterone levels (so, the more sex you have the more you will desire sex)

IMPORTANT NOTE REGARDING NATURAL APHRODISIACS

Some of these natural aphrodisiacs can be triggered at the same time depending on what you are doing. When you are physically active, e.g., sex, hiking, playing a physical game together you can have both dopamine, and oxytocin release in your body. That simply means you get double your pleasure.

So is there something that triggers all three basic 'love chemicals'? It appears that there is at least one thing that produces all three 'love chemicals'. When you make love your testosterone levels can be raised (this makes you desire sex), oxytocin is released which makes you feel trusting, closer and more attached, and your body also produces dopamine in your system which in turn produces a positive euphoria in your relationship ..... you feel excited about being in love.

> ## The Love Triple Play
>
> *Making love can produce all three of the major 'love chemicals'. This means that every time you make love you will desire sex more (testosterone), feel more trusting and attached (oxytocin), and you will be more excited...more euphoric about your love relationship (dopamine).*

Foundational Pillars

Step Six

Commitment to Relationship
Handout

Lack of Commitment

One of the greatest reasons that relationships fail or struggle is because divorce has become such an easy and acceptable alternative. It's almost as if it has become one of the most utilized strategies when couples are having difficulties. As long as we lack true commitment to making a relationship work the consuming flame of conflict will, in most cases, simply burn up any love feelings a person has for another. So, it is extremely important that you take a stand and say, "I am committed to this relationship no matter what, and I will do whatever is necessary to fix it." It's understood that there are some cases where someone is in danger that you must part. With this in mind what are the characteristics of commitment? What does it look like and what can you do to improve your personal commitment in your relationship?

Commitment in Relationships

True marriage commitment requires willingness to sacrifice (Nauert, R. 2012). In addition, Dr. Thomas Bradbury, co-director of the Relationship Institute, stated that, "A deeper level of commitment is a much better predictor of lower divorce rates and fewer problems in marriage. In a study that was done with 172 married couples they found that 78.5% of the couples who remained married were more committed. Below are four examples of what their deeper level of commitment looked like. The participants shared that these aspects of commitment helped them work through conflict and stay married.

- Each person in the relationship was resolved to make the relationship work.
- Each person was willing to make some sacrifices and take the steps needed to keep their relationship moving forward.
- Each person was committed to step up and take active steps to maintain their relationship, even if it meant he or she was not going to get his/her way in certain areas.
- Each person was willing to do what's difficult even when he/she didn't want to.

Couples who took on this level of commitment were more effective in solving their problems. The study also suggested that the couples in which both people were willing to make sacrifices for the sake of the marriage were significantly more likely to have lasting and happy marriages. So, commitment plays a huge role in not only maintaining the relationship, but also in the level of happiness that a couple can have.

> *A deeper level of commitment is a very good predictor of lower divorce rates and slower rates of deterioration in the relationship.*

Make Commitment to Your Relationship an Absolute

- You go out of your way to make sure your partner is happy and fulfilled in your relationship.
- You choose to be selfless instead of selfish in your relationship (you try to do what is best for the relationship).
- You are willing to sacrifice your wants, needs or desires occasionally for the betterment of your relationship.
- You take your partner into consideration and discuss options with him/her before you make plans for the future.
- You are willing to do what is difficult for the benefit of your relationship even when you don't feel like it.
- You enjoy having fun in your relationship and go out of your way to make it happen.
- If you had an important event scheduled and your partner got sick, you would stay home and take care of him/her.
- Success in your relationship is a priority over anything else in your life.
- When things get stressful or conflict arises in your relationship you initiate a discussion so that you can figure out how to fix things.
- Your partner is who you want in your life.
- You consistently put your partner's needs before your own.
- You consistently put your partner's needs before your friends and family.
- If an old flame contacted you and want to talk or hang out you would kindly say, 'No thanks, but I hope your life has gone well' (You would not meet with them or continue the conversation).
- You look forward to what life will bring to your relationship.
- You can't imagine living your life without your partner in it.
- When decisions are made regarding your future you make sure that your partner has a say in what happens.
- Regardless of the conflict, you put your relationship first. The best interests of the relationship comes before what you want.
- You are willing to step up and take active steps to maintain this relationship, even if it means you are not going to get your way in certain areas.
- Your relationship with your partner is a greater priority than anything else in your life.
- The decision to make this relationship work, no matter what, was made when you got married...or even before.

Make Your Partner Your Primary Priority
Handout

If your relationship is going to be what it is capable of becoming you must choose to put your partner first in your relationship. That simply means that your partner comes before your personal wants, needs, desires. Your partner comes before work. This is not suggesting that you don't work. However, you must keep in mind that your work is for the betterment of your relationship. If you spend too much time at work your priority is off. If you spend a lot of extra hours providing for your family you are probably not putting your partner first. One aspect of a sacrificial lover concept comes into play here. If you are to be a sacrificial lover in your relationship that means that you always consider how what you are choosing to do positively or negatively effects your partner. If it has a negative effect, you are not putting your partner first.

Make Your Partner Your Greatest Priority

- When my partner wants to talk, I put everything else to the side and take time to listen and share.
- When my partner calls me on the phone I immediately take time to see what he/she needs and speak with him/her.
- You kiss your partner goodbye each morning and say, "I love you".
- You great your partner and give him/her a kiss when you first meet after the work day.
- You attempt to hold hands when you are walking together.
- You try to make sure that you and your partner have at least one date night per week. If you are the man, you ask your wife out on a date once a week (don't just assume).
- You give your partner gifts or do things for him/her for no particular reason other than to show your love to him/her.
- You make sure to do special things for anniversary, birthdays or special events (flowers, gifts, dinner, etc.).
- When you are spending time with your partner and someone else calls, you let it go to voice mail.
- You initiate positive physical contact with your partner more than once daily for no reason other than to show love.
- When the two of us are at parties, church, work events, etc. you hold your partner's hand, put your around him/her, etc. to make sure other people know you are a couple.
- When you are at parties, church, work events, etc. you spend more time with your partner at your side than not.
- When you have important news, you share it with your partner first.
- You spend more time with your partner than anyone else socially.
- You make sure that you and your partner do fun things with each other weekly.
- You make sure that you and your partner have romantic time with each other at least once a week.
- You find ways to make your partner feel loved and fulfilled daily.

> *"Love is unfulfilled*
> *when you make anything else*
> *a higher priority."*

Becoming Service Oriented
Handout

Service is actually a powerful form of sacrificial love that can have tremendously positive effects on those who receive it. In the Greek language there is a word that is used for sacrificial or service love. It is agape. Agape love is a love that is unconditional and is consistently given in a selfless way. It is a commitment to seeking the best for the person you love without expectation of return. It does not change simply because the love is not returned. An interesting study was done at University of Fribourg in Switzerland. The results of their study showed that when both people in the relationship were willing to make sacrifices for the sake of the marriage they were significantly more likely to have lasting and happy marriages (Bradbury, Karney and Dominik Schoebi).

Serving your partner is really about developing an awareness of your partner's needs (how they are being overwhelmed at that given moment), and making a decision without being asked to simply do some things that will help him or her. The underlying purpose of serving your partner is to show your love by making his/her life easier at that specific moment in time. It is not responding to their every call, or sacrificing yourself entirely for their wants needs or desires. That becomes bondage instead of service and it extremely unhealthy. So what are some ways you could serve your partner? Let's take a look at a few possibilities.

> *Serving your spouse, doesn't mean beckoning to their every call. It means having a humble awareness of how you can help your partner and then taking action to do what needs to be done.*

Build Service Love into Your Relationship

- When your partner has more than (s)he can handle, ask if there is anything you could do to help at that moment in time.
- Do chores that you normally don't do when you see that they need to be done, e.g., vacuuming, doing the dishes, taking trash out, etc.
- Cook (or bring in food) when your partner is late or when (s)he is overwhelmed.
- At any moment in time simply do something that is normally your partner's responsibility just to be helpful.
- If you have kids, go out of your way to do something extra that your spouse may normally do. Help your kids with homework, getting ready for bed, bedtime chores, story time, family prayer, etc.
- Do little things for your partner and have no expectation of getting something back for it. Don't do these things to look good or for any other selfish reason.
- Try to do little things for your partner secretly and hope it has a positive impact on his/her life.
- Try to be creative in taking care of your partner without him/her asking.

Identify and Fulfill Primary Love Expectations

Step Seven

MARRIAGE GO ROUND ASSESSMENT

Name:_____ Date:_____

People are unique and as a result personal areas of concern vary from individual to individual. Below are listed some of the basic areas of concern that are most often suggested by individuals and couples when in therapy. Keep in mind that every person does not think that all of these areas of concern are important. Everyone is different and wants different things in order to feel loved. As a result, it is important that you very specifically define what areas are important to you so that your partner can learn how to better love you.

Top Six	Love Expectations	Area Defined	
	Change, partner is willing to change self	There must be a willingness to change as life occurs in a relationship. This is not changing your personality. It is looking within, or by listening to others, that you can identify ways that you can become a better person, how you can become a better partner.	
	Anger, Past Hurts and Irritants are addressed in a healthy way	Anger can cause significant difficulties in a relationship, as can past hurts and everyday irritants. It is essential that each person learn how to address these issues in his/her life and learn to be supportive of his/her partner as these issues are addressed.	
	Conflict Resolution or Management handled well	Problems and problem solving are just a normal part of life. We come to a resolution or compromise with our disagreements.	
	Forgiveness and Reconciliation occurs as needed	Forgiving others is important if you are to heal or at least improve a relationship. It is also important that you learn how to get forgiveness when you have offended someone. Learning to make recompense for reconciliation is important.	
	Emotionally Connected in relationship	Being emotionally connected calls for each person to identify what triggers positive emotional feelings in his/her partner and then do all you can to make sure those things happen often. Any positive emotional experience will cause you to feel closer to your partner.	
	Committed to Your Partner	Each person in the relationship has resolved to make the relationship work and is willing to make some sacrifices and take the steps needed to keep their relationship moving forward even when times are rough.	
	Priorities, Partner is primary or first priority	If you are to have a healthy relationship you must put your partner before children, personal time, work, friends, etc. Some people acknowledge that the only thing that should be above their partner is GOD.	

Top Six	Love Expectations	Area Defined	
	Service Love, Partner goes out of the way to serve you as needed	Serving your partner is really about developing an awareness of your partner's needs (how they are being overwhelmed at that given moment), and making a decision without being asked to simply help out. The underlying purpose of serving your partner is to show your love by making his/her life easier at that specific moment in time.	
	Admiration	You show admiration to someone who has positive characteristics worthy of adoration, love or respect. Admiration is a great motivator. When it is expressed it often is seen as a reward for well-doing or well-being.	
	Affection, Non-Sexual	Touching, hugs, holding hands, stroking hair, etc. are expressions of affection. Any non-sexual bonding experience that both enjoy, or that you can do to make your spouse feel loved and special.	
	Appreciation	You can show appreciation for your partner as you see them use their abilities for good or when they have done something for you or others. This can be done by patting them on the back, a gentle touch, a verbal thank you (be specific what it's for).	
	Attractive Partner	Most people like to spend time with people who are attractive and who do their best to look good. Looks aren't everything, but they are important for many people. How you look is often a reflection of your self-image. Men, being more visual, often need to have partners who take good care of themselves.	
	Commitment to Family	Both partners want the other to be a good mother, father and spouse. Putting the family first is often hard, but essential if a family is to be healthy.	
	Communication, Verbal	As human beings we all need communication. In most cases women need conversation in a relationship more than men do. It is very important that you take time to talk to each other on a daily basis.	
	Domestic Support	Either one or both people in a relationship may have a need to be helped regarding routine household duties. It should be an equal sharing of duties outside and inside when both work.	
	Emotional Security	Knowing that your spouse will protect you from emotional harm. This also means that your partner will seek not to emotionally abuse you, but rather lift you up as an important person in his/her life.	
	Finances	You have an agreement about how to spend money, how to pay the bills, how to save and how much each of you have for personal spending.	

Top Six	Love Expectations	Area Defined	
	Focused Attention	Focused attention simply means that when you are with your partner you focus on him/her. You listen, laugh, empathize, and generally make sure that (s)he knows that at that moment in time (s)he is the most important thing in the world to you.	
	Fun and Common Interests (having a recreational partner and friendships for socialization)	Having fun with someone you like being with is very bonding emotionally. It's important that you spend time having fun together. When you share common interests that both of you love doing it becomes even more positive and bonding for you in your relationship. This also includes the need for friendships to stimulate the relationship.	
	Goals, Marital	Together you have set goals for your marriage and you have worked toward those goals as a team.	
	Honesty	Honesty is the act of saying the truth whenever you are asked for it. Honesty never hides, it is an open book. However, honesty should also be gentle and kind.	
	Listening	Listening occurs when you, 1) listen for meaning or what your partner is trying to communicate, and 2) when you try to understand and see where your spouse is coming from, what they are thinking, and why they feel the way they do.	
	Openness	Openness occurs as you share what is going on inside of you as well as what has happened to you or around you on a day-by-day basis. Nothing should be hidden or kept from your partner. However, just as with honesty it should be shared in a gentle and kind way.	
	Personal Space	Everyone needs time alone! Time for relaxation, reading or simply enjoying a bath are essential if a person is going to feel good about self and have healthy relationships.	
	Physical Security	Knowledge that your spouse will take care of you, protect you and provide for your basic needs.	
	Priorities, Family	Establishing general priorities for marriage, family and self, are important. All of these priorities should be discussed with your partner so that you can mutually identify how these priorities can be worked and whether or not they are realistic.	
	Respect	To treat people in the manner in which you expect to be treated. To show consideration for another person. Acknowledgement, appreciation, recognition and consideration of another person's beliefs, knowledge, advice, etc. Verbal and non-verbal communication demonstrating that you value the other person.	
	Roles and Expectations	You have established roles in your relationship along with specific expectations for what each person's responsibilities.	

Top Six	Love Expectations	Area Defined	
	Romance	Romance usually implies some sort of expression of your strong romantic love for your partner. This includes a deep desire to connect with him/her intimately and is followed up by an effort to find creative ways in which you can express how much you appreciate and value your partner. Cards, flowers, going out to dinner, verbally sharing your love, etc. are all examples of being romantic.	
	Sexuality and Sexual Affection	Touching, hugs, caressing, etc. that are intended to be sexual teasers or foreplay techniques. This type of affection is used to help get your partner interested or ready for sexual activity. Sexually pleasuring your partner through intercourse, or other preferred methods of stimulation.	
	Spiritual Unity	Having a shared spiritual life is important to many couples. When so, each person in the relationship has certain spiritual expectations for the other. Defining what that is becomes important in the relationship.	
	Trust	Knowing that the other person will take care not to expose your weaknesses in a critical way. Once weaknesses are known, it is important that your partner not use them to hurt you in any way. This includes being open, honest, holding no secrets between each other. Emotional and physical affairs are the greatest breaches of trust.	

Marriage Go Round
Levels of Importance

Name:_____ Date:_____

Level 1: Essential   Level 2: Major Importance
Level 3: Moderate Importance   Level 4: Mild to Not too Important to me

Level 4

Level 3

Level 2

Level 1

Love Priority
Commitment
Service

Positive Emotions Activated
Foundational Core Issue

Conflict and Forgiveness
Cooling Down the Crisis

MARRIAGE GO ROUND
Alternative Partner Feedback Worksheet

Name: _____ Date:_____

Instructions: This exercise will help you and your partner identify how to improve identified areas that are most important to you in your relationship if you are to feel loved and cared for. It is not intended to be a list of do's and don'ts for your partner. Rather, it is information that validates what your partner is doing and what he or she could be doing that would make you feel better about your relationship. Often, due to lack of communication, whether it be sharing with or listening well, information is lost. This is a way of giving your partner information that can help him or her love you more the way you prefer to be loved.

1. To begin with look at the top six love expectations you have identified for you in the Marriage Go Round Assessment. Place them in hierarchical order beginning with your number one area. The name of the specific area of concern goes in the upper left hand corner of the left box.
2. In that left hand box list up to five bullet statements telling your partner how he or she is doing well in this particular area. You can have zero statements if your partner is not doing this well at all, or up to five statements if you can think of five objective things he or she does well in this specific area.
3. In the box on the right list up to five bullet statements telling your partner how he or she could better in this area. Be specific. Reproduce the next page for additional areas of concern that need to be addressed. Once you complete your top six you may choose to do all of the other areas as well.

How My Partner is Doing Well Now	How My Partner Could Do This Better for Me
_____	
_____	

How My Partner is Doing Well Now	How My Partner Could Do This Better for Me
_____	
_____	
_____	
_____	

Make copies of this page to complete additional areas!

Notes:

Identify and Address Secondary Love Expectations

Step Eight

MARRIAGE GO ROUND
Level Three Love Expectations

As previously stated people are unique and as a result each person may have specific love expectations that are unique to him or her. You have already identified your top six love expectations which were placed in the Marriage Go Round Levels of Importance chart (the top six were in level two). Now you need to list the level three love expectations in the place provided below.

1. List the level three love expectations that are important to you. Try to put them in hierarchical order (order of importance) if possible. Obviously your partner cannot do all of these things so make sure you put the ones that are most important to you at the top.
2. You do not have to list all of your level three expectations. Look at them closely and pick your top 5 to 10 level three love expectations and place them in the space provided below.
3. In the right hand column write down one thing your partner can do that meet this expectation in some way. Make it specific and behavioral.
4. Discuss these with your partner simply to let him or her know their importance to you.

	Secondary Love Expectation	Reason for Importance
1		
2		
3		
4		
5		
6		
7		
8		
9		
10		

Notes:

Abiding or Real Love Stage

Step Nine

Abiding or Real Love Stage Overview
Handout

Congratulations. You have accomplished a lot and have rekindled the love in your life. It takes work, but it is worth the effort. As you journey forward in your life together we would like for you to keep in mind the following:

Keep the Natural Love Drugs Flowing

By now you realize that these natural love drugs play a major role in the health and happiness that you can have in your relationship. There is one way to make sure that all three love chemicals stay in your body and have an ongoing impact on your relationship. Remember the Love Triple Play? Making love can produce all three of the major 'love chemicals'. This means that every time you make love:

1. You will desire sex more (testosterone),
2. Feel more trusting and attached (oxytocin),
3. You will be more excited…more euphoric about your love relationship (dopamine).

That is the easiest way to make sure that all three love drugs stay part of your lives. You can review the handout entitled, 'Natural Love Drugs: The Chemistry of Relationships' in order to see other ways you can stimulate those drugs in your body. Regardless of how you choose to stimulate them, just make sure it happens.

Conflict and Forgiveness Addressed

You have learned how to resolve or manage issues as they arise in your relationship. Make sure that you don't let little things go unnoticed and unmanaged. Make it a point to sit down weekly and air what needs to be addressed so conflict doesn't pile up on you. Also, maintain a humble attitude. If you mess up say, "I'm sorry." Go out of the way to make restitution if it is necessary and do all that you can to make things right when problems occur. If you were the offended accept the apology and what is done for restitution and let it go. Show love with compassion and treat your partner like you would like to be treated.

Positivity & Emotions Maintained

A love relationship must have positive emotions or the relationship is at risk. Remember to do the little things that will help you maintain your emotional closeness. Schedule time together, make sure it happens, and make it a priority to emotionally connect with your partner well and often. Men, ask your wives out on dates (women can do this also). Make sure that you have dates that are fun and dates that are romantic. Focus on your partner when you are out and any other time you are together. Talk, cuddle, flirt with each other. Have spontaneous sex, be passionate, and let your positive emotions come out showing your partner how special it is when you are together. Do everything you can to show your partner how important (s)he is to you. Share your feelings regarding how lucky you are to have such a wonderful partner. In order words, show your love daily in every way you can.

Foundational Pillars Fulfilled (level 1)

You need to be thinking about how you can make the Foundational Pillars part of your everyday life. It is very important that you incorporate these three key pillars into how you treat your partner daily.

- Putting your partner first: Constantly remind your partner by words and deeds that (s)he is the most important thing in your life. Nothing other than GOD will remove him or her from being in first place.

- Committing to your relationship: Weekly let your partner know that you are in this relationship and don't ever plan on leaving. You want to live out your years with the love of your life and whether there are bumpy times or not your love will endure.
- Serving your partner: Always be on the lookout for ways to help your partner when (s)he is stressed, overwhelmed, etc. Find ways to help so that you can have more quality time together.

Primary Love Expectations Met (level 2)

Please keep in mind that just because you have recently identified love expectations while in therapy doesn't mean that you are done. It is very important that you communicate with each other to assure that you are getting your love expectations met. Life, children, work, etc. can all get in the way and cause you to forget or put these important parts of your marriage on the back burner. Don't let that happen.

Secondary (level 3 & 4) Love Expectations Reviewed and Addressed as Needed

Don't forget to look at the secondary love expectations. Although they may not be nearly as important as the primary love expectations you can still periodically go out of your way to address them. Look over your partners 'Marriage Go Round Levels of Importance' chart to help you remember what is primary and what may also be important that is secondary in nature. Review this information weekly as a reminder as to how you can show love in a more effective way to your partner. Periodically ask if there is something else that you can do that would make your partner feel even more loved. The benefits certainly outweigh the effort involved. Enjoy!

Rules for Positive Partnering
Handout

It is important that you remain emotionally present instead of fighting or running when things get bad. When you remain emotionally present you have a much better chance at resolving or managing issues as they arise. There are a number of actions you can take that will help you stay emotionally present when things get tough. Some of them are as follows:

Commit to your relationship and let your partner know that no matter how hard it gets you are in it for the long hall. You believe that there is nothing more important than your relationship and will do whatever it takes to manage or resolve conflict.

Make sure that your partner knows that other than GOD (s)he is the number one priority in your life, and show it by your words and actions.

Build service orientation into your relationship. If your partner sees that you are seeking to serve or help out when things are difficult it makes for a better relationship.

Maintain a positive emotional connection. Show by words and deeds that you love your partner and want the best for him/her.

Make sure that trust and forgiveness is your default mode in your relationship. When you do this, it makes it much easier to address disagreements with minimal issues.

Constantly seek to maintain a positivity in your relationship. Being positive and constructive can go along ways in addressing conflict and in showing love, compassion, etc. If one of you bring negativity to the situation the other must work hard at redirecting things so that you can start to experience a positive interaction again.

Respect one another unconditionally. Even when upset, couples should still be able to express their feelings with respect.

Stay focused on solutions not problems. Believe it or not, it's not uncommon for partners to spend months, even years, on one or two unresolved issues. Individuals in a positive relationship identify the problem and then focus their energy on generating solutions and following up with actions.

Be open-minded and flexible. Being open to new possibilities and flexible to change when needed produces positive benefits for the relationship.

Be positive in your relationship. See your partner in a positive light as much as is possible. When you do it makes it easier for you to respond to each other with empathy which in turn enhances a stronger foundation for your relationship.

Laugh and have fun with each other often. When you play together and laugh it is very bonding. It causes you to want to be close to your partner.

Focus on what your partner does right, not what he or she does wrong. Couples who focus on the positive have a happier, stronger relationship.

The Key to Ongoing Success

The Key to ongoing Success Is to Repeat Steps One Through Nine on a Consistent Basis!

Couple Concerns
Post Assessment

Name:_____ Date:_____

Instructions: Look at each of the potential issues listed below and rate whether or not each one is an issue in any way for you or your partner in your relationship. You are not rating your partner. You are rating if any of these areas are causing a problem for either of you in the relationship. There are empty spots at the end. Look back at your initial Couple Concerns Pre-Assessment. Add any concerns that you had on that assessment before you do this post assessment.

1 = No problem   2 = Mild Problem   3 = Moderate Problem   4 = Significant Problem

	Relationship Concerns	Area Defined	Rating
1	Change, a willingness to change self	There must be a willingness to change as life occurs in a relationship, This is not changing your personality. It is looking within, or by listening to others, so that you can identify ways that you can become a better person, how you can become a better partner.	1 2 3 4
2	Anger, Past Hurts and Irritants	Anger can cause significant difficulties in a relationship, as can past hurts and everyday irritants. It is essential that each person learn how to address these issues in his/her life and learn to be supportive of his/her partner as these issues are addressed.	1 2 3 4
3	Conflict Resolution or Management	Problems and problem solving are just a normal part of life. We come to a resolution or compromise with our disagreements.	1 2 3 4
4	Forgiveness and Reconciliation	Forgiving others is important if you are to heal or at least improve a relationship. It is also important that you learn how to get forgiveness when you have offended someone. Learning to make recompense for reconciliation is important.	1 2 3 4
5	Emotional Connection	Being emotionally connected calls for each person to identify what triggers positive emotional feelings in his/her partner and then do all you can to make sure those things happen often. Any positive emotional experience will cause you to feel closer to your partner.	1 2 3 4
6	Commitment to Partner	Each person in the relationship has resolved to make the relationship work and is willing to make some sacrifices and take the steps needed to keep their relationship moving forward even when times are rough.	1 2 3 4
7	Priorities, Partner	If you are to have a healthy relationship you must put your partner before children, personal time, work, friends, etc. Some people acknowledge that the only thing that should be above their partner is GOD.	1 2 3 4
8	Service Love	Serving your partner is really about developing an awareness of your partner's needs (how they are being overwhelmed at that given moment), and making a decision without being asked to simply help out. The underlying purpose of serving your partner is to show your love by making his/her life easier at that specific moment in time.	1 2 3 4

9	Admiration	You show admiration to someone who has positive characteristics worthy of adoration, love or respect. Admiration is a great motivator. When it is expressed it often is seen as a reward for well-doing or well-being.	1 2 3 4
10	Affection, Non-Sexual	Touching, hugs, holding hands, stroking hair, etc. are expressions of affection. Any non-sexual bonding experience that both enjoy, or that you can do to make your spouse feel loved and special.	1 2 3 4
11	Appreciation	You can show appreciation for your partner as you see them use their abilities for good or when they have done something for you or others. This can be done by patting them on the back, a gentle touch, a verbal thank you (be specific what it's for).	1 2 3 4
12	Attractive Partner	Most people like to spend time with people who are attractive and who do their best to look good. Looks aren't everything, but they are important for many people. How you look is often a reflection of your self-image. Men, being more visual, often need to have partners who take good care of themselves.	1 2 3 4
13	Commitment to Family	Both partners want the other to be a good mother, father and spouse. Putting the family first is often hard but essential if a family is to be healthy.	1 2 3 4
14	Communication, Verbal	As human beings we all need communication. In most cases women need conversation in a relationship more than men do. It is very important that you take time to talk to each other on a daily basis.	1 2 3 4
15	Domestic Support	Either one or both people in a relationship may have a need to be helped regarding routine household duties. It should be an equal sharing of duties outside and inside when both work.	1 2 3 4
16	Emotional Security	Knowing that your spouse will protect you from emotional harm. This also means that your partner will seek not to emotionally abuse you but rather lift you up as an important person in his/her life.	1 2 3 4
17	Finances	You have an agreement about how to spend money, how to pay the bills, how to save and how much each of you have for personal spending.	1 2 3 4
18	Focused Attention	Focused attention simply means that when you are with your partner you focus on him/her. You listen, laugh, empathize, and generally make sure that (s)he knows that at that moment in time (s)he is the most important thing in the world to you	1 2 3 4
19	Fun and Common Interests (having a recreational partner and friendships for socialization)	Having fun with someone you like being with is very bonding emotionally. It's important that you spend time having fun together. When you share common interests that both of you love doing it becomes even more positive and bonding for you in your relationship. This also includes the need for friendships to stimulate the relationship.	1 2 3 4
20	Goals, Marital	Together you have set goals for your marriage and you have worked toward those goals as a team.	1 2 3 4
21	Honesty	Honesty is the act of saying the truth whenever you are asked for it. Honesty never hides, it is an open book. However, honesty should also be gentle and kind.	1 2 3 4

22	Listening	Listening occurs when you, 1) listen for meaning or what your partner is trying to communicate, and 2) when you try to understand and see where your spouse is coming from, what they are thinking, and why they feel the way they do.	1 2 3 4
23	Openness	Openness occurs as you share what is going on inside of you as well as what has happened to you or around you on a day-by-day basis. Nothing should be hidden or kept from your partner. However, just as with honesty it should be shared in a gentle and kind way.	1 2 3 4
24	Personal Space	Everyone needs time alone! Time for relaxation, reading or simply enjoying a bath are essential if a person is going to feel good about self and have healthy relationships.	1 2 3 4
25	Physical Security	Knowledge that your spouse will take care of you, protect you and provide for your basic needs.	1 2 3 4
26	Priorities, Family	Establishing general priorities for marriage, family and self, are important. All of these priorities should be discussed with your partner so that you can mutually identify how these priorities can be worked and whether or not they are realistic.	1 2 3 4
27	Respect	To treat people in the manner in which you expect to be treated. To show consideration for another person. Acknowledgement, appreciation, recognition and consideration of another person's beliefs, knowledge, advice, etc. Verbal and non-verbal communication demonstrating that you value the other person.	1 2 3 4
28	Roles and Expectations	You have established roles in your relationship along with specific expectations for each person's responsibilities.	1 2 3 4
29	Romance	Romance usually implies some sort of expression of your strong romantic love for your partner. This includes a deep desire to connect with him/her intimately and is followed up by an effort to find creative ways in which you can express how much you appreciate and value your partner. Cards, flowers, going out to dinner, verbally sharing your love, etc. are all examples of being romantic.	1 2 3 4
30	Sexuality and Sexual Affection	Touching, hugs, caressing, etc. that are intended to be sexual teasers or foreplay techniques. This type of affection is used to help get your partner interested or ready for sexual activity that might lead to sexual intercourse, or other preferred methods of stimulation.	1 2 3 4
31	Spiritual Unity	Having a shared spiritual life is important to many couples. When so, each person in the relationship has certain spiritual expectations for the other. Defining what that is becomes important in the relationship.	1 2 3 4
32	Trust	Knowing that the other person will take care not to expose your weaknesses in a critical way. Once weaknesses are known, it is important that your partner not use them to hurt you in any way. This includes being open, honest, holding no secrets between each other. Emotional and physical affairs are the greatest breaches of trust.	1 2 3 4
33			1 2 3 4
34			1 2 3 4
35			1 2 3 4

NOTES:

Other Materials Written by this Author

www.critescounseling.com

Marriage Go Round the First Journey (Therapist Manual)

Bipolar or ADHD: Educational and Home Based Strategies for Bipolar Disorder, ADHD and other Co-Existing Conditions

Executive Function Disorder: Educational/Behavioral Strategies for ADHD, Bipolar, Asperger and other Brain Based Disorders

Family Therapy Manual: A Pragmatic Approach to Family Therapy

Pragmatic Therapy: Counseling Individuals Who Come From Dysfunctional Families

Programs

Russ has led Marriage Enrichment Programs for over thirty years. He is available for:

- Half Day Marriage Go Round programs
- One day Marriage Go Round workshops
- Marriage Go Round Weekend retreats

Call 972-506-7111 for more information.

www.ingramcontent.com/pod-product-compliance
Lightning Source LLC
Chambersburg PA
CBHW081230280526
45787CB00006B/2600